Envision It! | Visual Skills Handbook

Realism and Fantasy

Literary Elements

Realism and Fantasy

Realism

Fantasy

Literary Elements

Characters

Setting

Plot

Envision It! Visual Strategies Handbook

Background Knowledge

Important Ideas

Inferring

Monitor and Clarify

Predict and Set Purpose

Questioning

Story Structure

Summarize

Text Structure

Visualize

Background Knowledge

Let's Think About Reading!

- What do I already know?
- What does this remind me of?

Important Ideas

Let's Think About Reading!

- What is important to know?

Inferring

Let's Think About Reading!

- What do I already know?
- How does this help me understand what happened?

Monitor and Clarify

Let's Think About Reading!

- What does not make sense?
- How can I fix it?

Predict and Set Purpose

Let's Think About Reading!

- What do I already know?
- What do I think will happen?
- What is my purpose for reading?

Questioning

Let's Think About Reading!

- What questions do I have about what I am reading?

Story Structure

Let's Think About Reading!

- What happens in the beginning?
- What happens in the middle?
- What happens in the end?

Summarize

Let's Think About Reading!

- What happens in the story?
- What is the story mainly about?

Text Structure

Let's Think About Reading!

- How is the story organized?
- Are there any patterns?

Visualize

Let's Think About Reading!

- What pictures do I see in my mind?

SCOTT FORESMAN

READING STREET

GRADE 1

COMMON CORE ©

Program Authors

Peter Afflerbach
Camille Blachowicz
Candy Dawson Boyd
Elena Izquierdo
Connie Juel
Edward Kame'enui
Donald Leu
Jeanne R. Paratore
P. David Pearson
Sam Sebesta
Deborah Simmons
Susan Watts Taffe
Alfred Tatum
Sharon Vaughn
Karen Kring Wixson

Glenview, Illinois
Boston, Massachusetts
Chandler, Arizona
Hoboken, New Jersey

ALWAYS LEARNING PEARSON

We dedicate Reading Street to
Peter Jovanovich.

His wisdom, courage,
and passion for education
are an inspiration to us all.

Acknowledgments appear on page 176, which constitutes an extension of this copyright page.

ISBN-13: 978-0-328-72443-7
ISBN-10: 0-328-72443-2
9 10 11 12 13 14 15 16 17 18 V011 18 17 16 15 14

Dear Reader,

A new school year is beginning. Are you ready? You are about to take a trip along a famous street—*Scott Foresman Reading Street.* On this trip you will meet a dog named Tam, a cat named Tip, and boys and girls just like you!

As you read the stories and articles, you will gain exciting new information that will help you in science and social studies.

While you're enjoying these exciting pieces of literature, you will find that something else is going on—you are becoming a better reader by gaining new skills and polishing old ones.

Have a great trip, and send us a postcard!

Sincerely,
The Authors

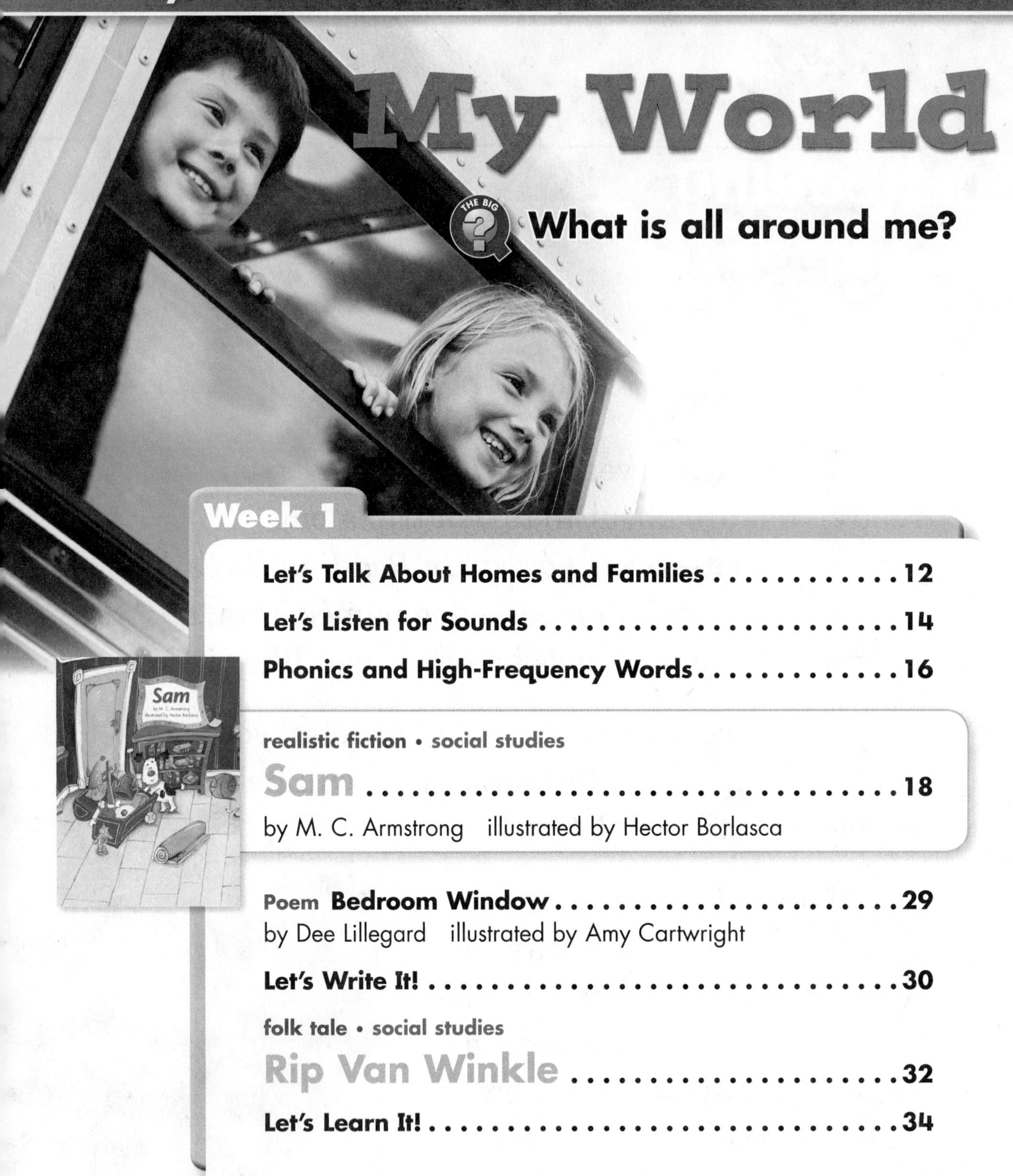

My World

THE BIG ? **What is all around me?**

Week 1

Week 2

Week 3

Ready, Set, Read! Contents

Week 4

Week 5

Week 6

Envision It! A Comprehension Handbook

Don Leu
The Internet Guy

Right before our eyes, the nature of reading and learning is changing. The Internet and other technologies create new opportunities, new solutions, and new literacies. New reading comprehension skills are required online. They are increasingly important to our students and our society.

Those of us on the Reading Street team are here to help you on this new, and very exciting, journey.

See It!

- Big Question Video
- Concept Talk Video

- Envision It! Animations
- eReaders

- Interactive Sound-Spelling Cards

Hear It!

- *Sing with Me* Animations
- eSelections
- Grammar Jammer

- Vocabulary Activities

Concept Talk Video

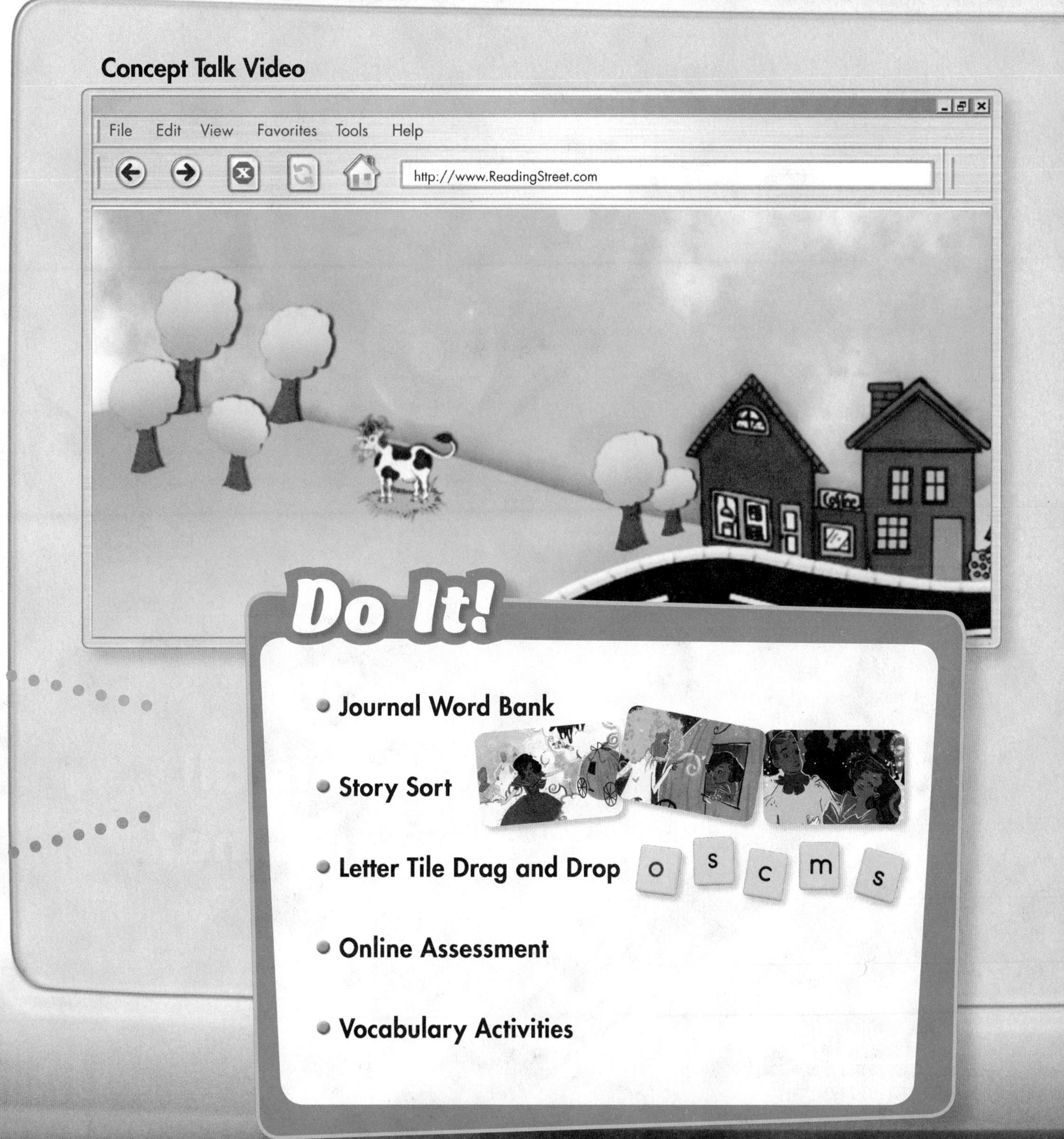

Ready, Set, Read!

My World

What is all around me?

Reading Street Online

www.ReadingStreet.com

- Big Question Video
- eSelections
- Envision It! Animations
- Story Sort

Common Core State Standards
Language 5.c. Identify real-life connections between words and their use (e.g., note places at home that are *cozy*).

Oral Vocabulary

Let's Talk About

Read Together

Homes and Families

- Share information about life at home.
- Share ideas about what is around us at home.

READING STREET ONLINE
CONCEPT TALK VIDEO
www.ReadingStreet.com

You will learn
2 8 1
Amazing Words
this year!

Common Core State Standards
Foundational Skills 2.c. Isolate and pronounce initial, medial vowel, and final sounds (phonemes) in spoken single-syllable words.

Let's Listen for

Sounds

Read Together

- Find five things that begin with the sound /m/. Say the beginning sound.
- Find three things that end with the sound /s/. Say the ending sound.
- Find three things that begin with the sound /t/.
- Find something that begins with the short *a* sound. Say each sound in the word.

READING STREET ONLINE
SOUND-SPELLING CARDS
www.ReadingStreet.com

Monday
17
7+2
3-2
1+4
6-1
5+3

Common Core State Standards
Foundational Skills 2.c. Isolate and pronounce initial, medial vowel, and final sounds (phonemes) in spoken single-syllable words. **Also Foundational Skills 3., 3.g.**

Phonics

Consonants *m, s, t;* Short *a*

Words I Can Blend

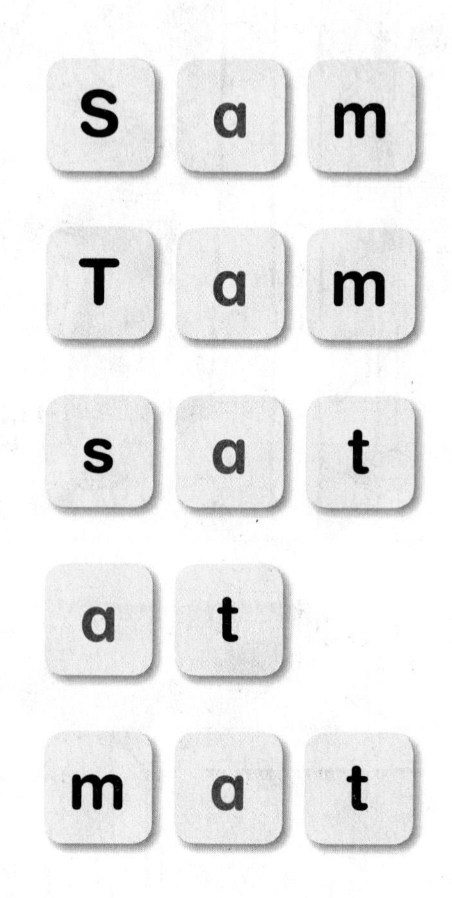

High-Frequency Words

Words I Can Read

see

green

Sentences I Can Read

1. I see Sam.
2. Tam sat.
3. Sam sat at a green mat.

You've learned

- Consonants *m, s, t*
- Short *a*

High-Frequency Words

I see a green

Sam

by M. C. Armstrong
illustrated by Hector Borlasca

Genre

Realistic fiction is a kind of story. It is made up, but it is about things that could be real.

Question of the Week

What is around us at home?

I am Sam. Am I Sam?

I am Tam. Am I Tam?

See Tam. Tam sat.

Sam sat. Sam sat at a mat.

Sam sat at a green mat.

Sam sat. Tam sat.

Am I Sam? Am I Tam?

Sam sat. Tam sat.

Think Critically

1. What do you already know about dogs that helps you understand what Tam does? **Text to Self**

2. What can you learn about Sam by reading the story? **Character**

3. **Look Back and Write** Look back at page 21. Where is Tam? Write the things you see.

Key Ideas and Details • Text Evidence

Bedroom Window

Sun rises
Lights the sky
Shines through
the window's eye.

by Dee Lillegard
illustrated by Amy Cartwright

Common Core State Standards
Language 1.c. Use singular and plural nouns with matching verbs in basic sentences (e.g., *He hops; We hop*). **Also Language 5.a.**

Key Features of Nouns in Sentences

- tell about people, animals, and things
- help tell the idea of the sentence

READING STREET ONLINE
GRAMMAR JAMMER
www.ReadingStreet.com

Narrative

Nouns in Sentences

A **sentence** is a group of words that tells a complete idea. Words that name people, animals, or things are **nouns**. Most sentences have nouns.

Writing Prompt Think about a pet you would like. Write a sentence about the pet. Name the animal in your sentence.

Writer's Checklist

Remember, you should ...

- ✓ write about an animal.
- ✓ name the animal in your sentence.
- ✓ begin the sentence with an uppercase, or capital, letter.

Student Model

A cat can run.

I like a cat.

Each sentence starts with an uppercase, or capital, letter.

Each **sentence** tells a complete idea.

The **noun** **cat** names an animal.

Conventions

Nouns: People, Animals, and Things

Remember Some words name people, animals, or things. Naming words are called **nouns.** **Man, cup,** and **cat** are nouns. What nouns can you think of that name people, animals, or things?

Common Core State Standards
Literature 3. Describe characters, settings, and major events in a story, using key details. **Also Literature 5., 7.**

Social Studies in Reading

Read Together

Genre
Folk Tale

- A folk tale is a story that people have told again and again through the years. Folk tales began as oral stories, or stories that were told. Later, they were written down.
- A folk tale often begins with the phrase "Long ago." This phrase shows that the story is an old one.
- A folk tale is usually a well-known story. Sometimes the meaning of a folk tale can be connected to a reader's personal experiences.
- Read "Rip Van Winkle." Think about what makes it a folk tale.

Rip Van Winkle

Long ago, Rip Van Winkle climbed up a hill. He fell asleep.

Rip slept for many years! He told his story again and again. People liked to hear the story.

Let's **Think** About...

This story begins with the phrase "Long ago." What does that tell you? **Folk Tale**

Let's **Think** About...

How can you connect what happened to Rip to something that has happened to you? **Folk Tale**

Let's **Think** About...

Reading Across Texts Tell what Sam does in *Sam*. Tell what Rip does in "Rip Van Winkle." Which actions could really happen?

Writing Across Texts Imagine Rip tells his story to Sam. What does Sam think of the story? Write about what Sam thinks.

Common Core State Standards
Speaking/Listening 1.a. Follow agreed-upon rules for discussions (e.g., listening to others with care, speaking one at a time about the topics and texts under discussion). **Also Foundational Skills 3.g., Language 1.a.**

Read Together

Let's Learn It!

READING STREET ONLINE
VOCABULARY ACTIVITIES
www.ReadingStreet.com

Listening and Speaking

Follow agreed-upon rules in a group discussion.

Participate in a Discussion When we work in a group, we follow rules of discussion. We listen to each other and talk when someone calls our name. We stay on topic.

Practice It! Think about the story you read this week—*Sam*. Follow the rules. Listen to others. Take turns telling about something you liked in the story. Use nouns as you speak.

Vocabulary

A **noun** is a word that names a person, an animal, a place, or a thing. We can sort nouns into groups.

These nouns are all names for animals.

Practice It! Read these words. Sort them into categories of people, animals, places, or things.

boy **bus** **girl** **home** **tree**

Handwriting

Proper Body Position Be sure to sit up straight when you write. Write neatly, from left to right and from top to bottom. Look at the models on pages 174–175. Then write a row of these letters:

Mm **Tt** **Ss** **Aa**

Common Core State Standards
Language 5.c. Identify real-life connections between words and their use (e.g., note places at home that are *cozy*).

Oral Vocabulary

Let's Talk About

Read Together

Homes and Families

- Share information about families.
- Share ideas about who is in our families.

READING STREET ONLINE
CONCEPT TALK VIDEO
www.ReadingStreet.com

You've learned
0 0 7
Amazing Words
so far this year!

- Find five things that begin with the sound /p/. Say the beginning sound.
- Find two things that rhyme with *fan*. Say the ending sound.
- Find five things that begin with the sound /n/.
- Find something that rhymes with *map*. Say each sound in the word.

READING STREET ONLINE
SOUND-SPELLING CARDS
www.ReadingStreet.com

HARDWARE
204
KITCHEN SUPPLIES
202
FRUIT
SALE

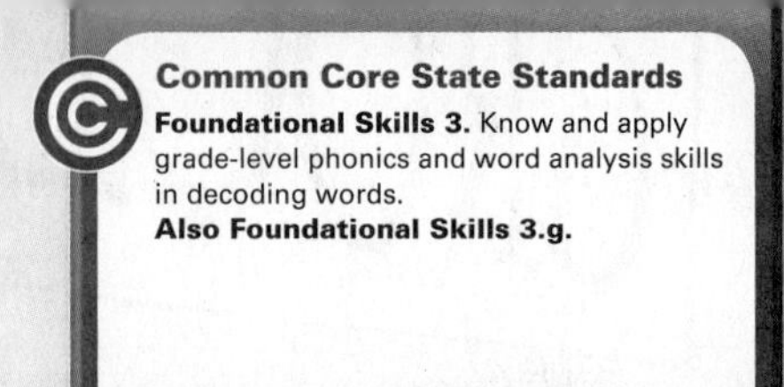

Phonics

Consonants *c, p*

Words I Can Blend

Words I Can Read

like

one

the

Sentences I Can Read

1. We pat one cat.
2. I like a cap.
3. Sam, tap the map.

Common Core State Standards
Foundational Skills 3. Know and apply grade-level phonics and word analysis skills in decoding words.
Also Foundational Skills 3.g.

Phonics

Consonant *n*

Words I Can Blend

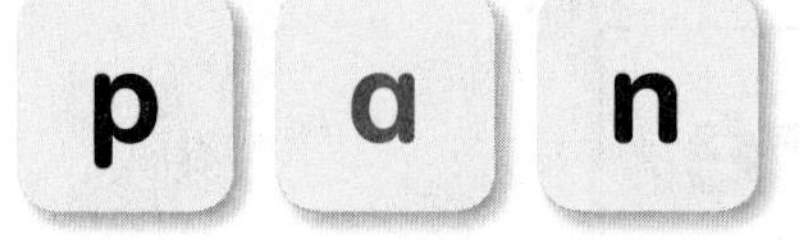

t a n

I Can Read!

One tan cat sat. Sam can pat the tan cat. Matt can pat the tan cat.

We like Sam. We like Matt. We like the tan cat. The tan cat can nap.

Nap, tan cat! Nap!

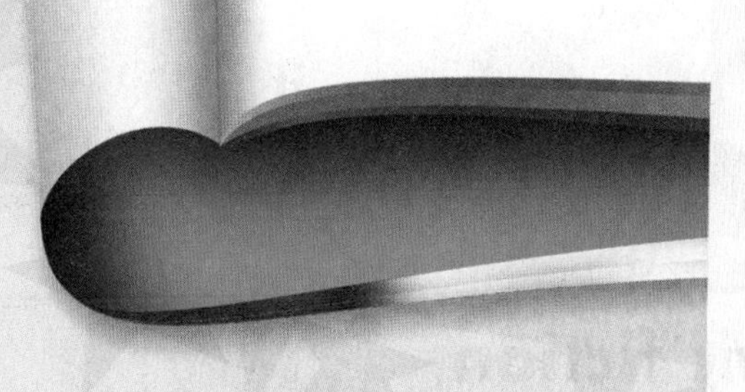

You've learned

Consonants *c, p, n*

High-Frequency Words

we like one the

Snap!

by Jacqui Briggs
illustrated by Hector Borlasca

Genre Stories that are **realistic fiction** happen in a place that seems real. In this story, Sam's house might be like a house near you.

Question of the Week
Who is in our family?

I am Sam.

I can tap one pan.

Pam can tap at the tan mat.

Tap, Pam, tap!

Tap, tap, tap! We can tap!

Tam sat. I can pat Tam.

Pat, pat, pat!

Pam can pat Tam.

Pat, pat, pat!

I see Mac. We like Mac.

Mac can snap.

Mac can snap.

Snap, snap, snap!

Snap Pam. Snap Sam.

Tam can nap. Snap, snap!

Common Core State Standards
Literature 1. Ask and answer questions about key details in a text. **Also Literature 2., Writing 3.**

Envision It! | Retell

READING STREET ONLINE
STORY SORT
www.ReadingStreet.com

Think Critically

1. What does Mac do? Where else might someone like Mac work? Text to World

2. Where does this story happen? Setting

3. **Look Back and Write**
   Look back at pages 51 and 52. Who comes to Sam's house? Write about what this person does.

   Key Ideas and Details • Text Evidence

My Family

Part of my family is
grown-up and tall.

Part of my family is
little and small.

I'm in the middle
and pleased with them all.

by Marchette Chute
illustrated by Wednesday Kirwan

Common Core State Standards
Language 1.c. Use singular and plural nouns with matching verbs in basic sentences (e.g., *He hops; We hop*).

Key Features of Nouns in Sentences

- can tell about places
- help tell the idea of the sentence

READING STREET ONLINE
GRAMMAR JAMMER
www.ReadingStreet.com

Narrative

Nouns in Sentences

A **sentence** is a group of words that tells a complete idea. A noun in a sentence can name a place, such as a *store, park,* or *house.*

Writing Prompt Think about a place you go during the day. Write about the place. Tell the name of the place in your sentence.

Writer's Checklist

Remember, you should . . .

- ✓ tell about a place to go.
- ✓ name the place in your sentence.
- ✓ end your sentence with a period.

Student Model

My mom and I walk to the store.

The sentence tells a complete idea.

The **noun store** names a place.

A **period** ends the sentence.

Conventions

Nouns: Places

Remember Some nouns name places. **Room, store,** and **park** are all nouns that name places. What other nouns can you think of that name places?

farm

school

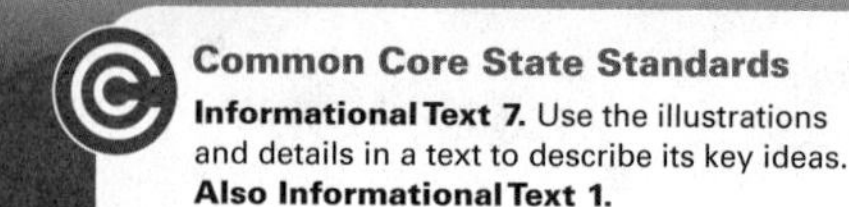

Common Core State Standards
Informational Text 7. Use the illustrations and details in a text to describe its key ideas. **Also Informational Text 1.**

Social Studies in Reading

Read Together

Genre
Photo Essay

- The word *photo* is a short way to say *photograph*.
- A photo essay is made up of photographs and words. The photographs help explain the words.
- All the photographs and words in a photo essay are about the same topic.
- Read "Families." As you read, look for elements of a photo essay. Ask yourself questions about the text.

Families

A family is a group of people who love each other.

Families play together.
Families eat together.

Families read together.
What does your family like to do together?

Let's **Think** About...

What do these photographs show about the topic of families? What questions do you have?
Photo Essay

Let's **Think** About...

Reading Across Texts How are photographs important in both *Snap!* and "Families"?

Writing Across Texts Draw pictures of a family from each selection doing something together. Write a sentence that tells about each picture.

Common Core State Standards
Speaking/Listening 1.a. Follow agreed-upon rules for discussions (e.g., listening to others with care, speaking one at a time about the topics and texts under discussion). **Also Language 1.a., 1.f.**

READING STREET ONLINE
VOCABULARY ACTIVITIES
www.ReadingStreet.com

Cass and I had our picture taken. Mac took the picture.

Share ideas by telling about something that happened.

Share Ideas When we tell others about things that we do, we make sure to speak clearly. We tell about what happened and how it happened.

Practice It! Think of something that happened to you. Tell others about it. Speak clearly and slowly. Use a noun for each person, place, or thing that you mention.

Vocabulary

A descriptive word, or **adjective,** is a word that tells about people, places, animals, or things.

***Green* and *tall* are words that describe the tree.**

Practice It! Think about an apple. Choose words that might describe it.

green **red** **shiny** **funny**

Handwriting

Proper Letter Size When you write, it should be easy to tell the difference between letters that are tall, letters that are small, and letters that fall. Write neatly, from left to right and from top to bottom. Look at the models on pages 174–175. Then write a row of these letters: **Cc** **Pp** **Nn**

Common Core State Standards
Language 5.c. Identify real-life connections between words and their use (e.g., note places at home that are *cozy*).

Oral Vocabulary

Let's Talk About

Read Together

Homes and Families

- Share information about life outside at home.
- Share ideas about what is outside our door.

READING STREET ONLINE
CONCEPT TALK VIDEO
www.ReadingStreet.com

You've learned
0 1 4
Amazing Words
so far this year!

Common Core State Standards
Foundational Skills 2.c. Isolate and pronounce initial, medial vowel, and final sounds (phonemes) in spoken single-syllable words.

Phonemic Awareness

Let's Listen for

Read Together

Sounds

- Find five things that begin with the sound /f/. Say the sound.
- Find five things that begin with the sound /b/. Say the sound.
- Find three things that end with the sound /g/. Say the sound.
- Find something that rhymes with *wall*. Say each sound in the word.
- Find three things that contain the short *i* sound.

READING STREET ONLINE
SOUND-SPELLING CARDS
www.ReadingStreet.com

Common Core State Standards
Foundational Skills 3.b. Decode regularly spelled one-syllable words. **Also Foundational Skills 3.g.**

Phonics

Consonants *f, b*

Words I Can Blend

b a t

n a b

c a b

Words I Can Read

was

yellow

do

you

look

Sentences I Can Read

1. One fan was yellow.
2. Do you see the fat bat?
3. Look at Cass nab a cab.

Common Core State Standards
Foundational Skills 3.b. Decode regularly spelled one-syllable words. **Also Foundational Skills 3.g.**

Phonics

Consonant *g*, Short *i*

Words I Can Blend

b a g

p i g

p i n

i t

I Can Read!

A yellow pig sat in a big bin.

Look at it, Tim. Do you see it? A pig can sit in the big bin. A fat cat can sit in the big bin.

It was a big, big bin.

- Consonants *f, b, g*
- Short *i*

High-Frequency Words

was yellow do you look

Tip and Tam

by Mary-Nell Lee
illustrated by Hector Borlasca

Realistic fiction tells about things that could really happen, but the stories are made up. Next you will read about friends who are made-up characters.

Question of the Week

What is outside our door?

Nan can tap Sam.

Pat can tap Pam.

Sam can tap Pat.

Pam can tap Nan.

Do you see Tip?

Look at the yellow cat.

Tip can bat the big tan bag.

Tam can nip at it.

Tam can sit in the big bag!

Tip can fit in it.

Can Pam see Tip?

Can Sam see Tam?

Look at the fat tan bag!

Tip was in the big tan bag!

Tam sat in it!

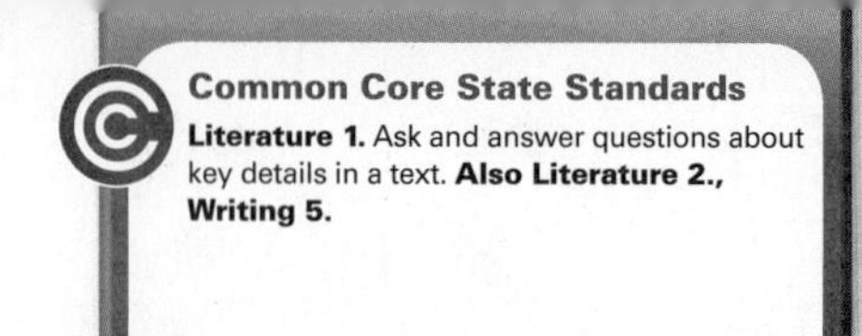

Envision It! | Retell

Think Critically

1. What are Sam and his friends doing in the yard? What have you seen people doing in their yards? Text to Self

2. What happens at the end of the story? Why is it important? Plot

3. **Look Back and Write** Look back at page 79. Where are Tip and Tam? Write about how you know.

Key Ideas and Details • Text Evidence

Home

All around me quiet.
All around me peaceful.
All around me lasting.
All around me home.

Ute Indian poem
illustrated by Susan Mitchell

Common Core State Standards
Language 1.e. Use verbs to convey a sense of past, present, and future (e.g., *Yesterday I walked home; Today I walk home; Tomorrow I will walk home*).

Key Features of Verbs in Sentences

- tell about what we do
- help tell the idea of the sentence

READING STREET ONLINE
GRAMMAR JAMMER
www.ReadingStreet.com

Verbs in Sentences

A **sentence** tells a complete idea. Some words in sentences tell what we do. Words that tell actions are **verbs**. All sentences have verbs.

Writing Prompt Think about something you do with friends. Write about what you and your friends do. Use a verb in your sentence.

Writer's Checklist

Remember, you should . . .

- ✓ write about something you do with friends.
- ✓ use a verb in your sentence.
- ✓ begin the sentence with an uppercase, or capital, letter.

Student Model

We play games.

This sentence begins with an uppercase, or capital, *W*.

The **sentence** tells what the writer and other children do.

The **verb play** tells about an action.

Conventions

Verbs

Remember Some words are action words. Action words are called **verbs**. Verbs tell what we do. **Run, talk,** and **play** are verbs. What verbs can you say?

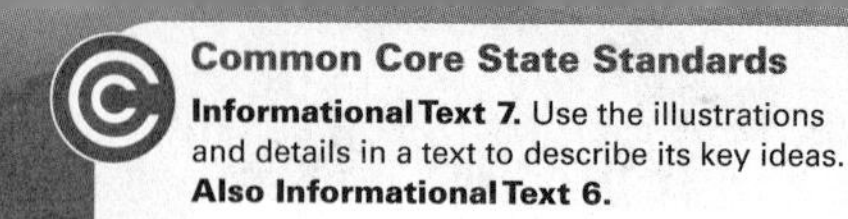

Common Core State Standards
Informational Text 7. Use the illustrations and details in a text to describe its key ideas. **Also Informational Text 6.**

Read Together

Genre
Photo Essay

- In a photo essay, photographs and words work together to tell about one topic.
- A photo essay may inform or entertain readers.
- Photo essays show real people, places, and events. They can be photographs from the past or from the present.
- As you read "Yards," think about what makes it a photo essay.

Yards

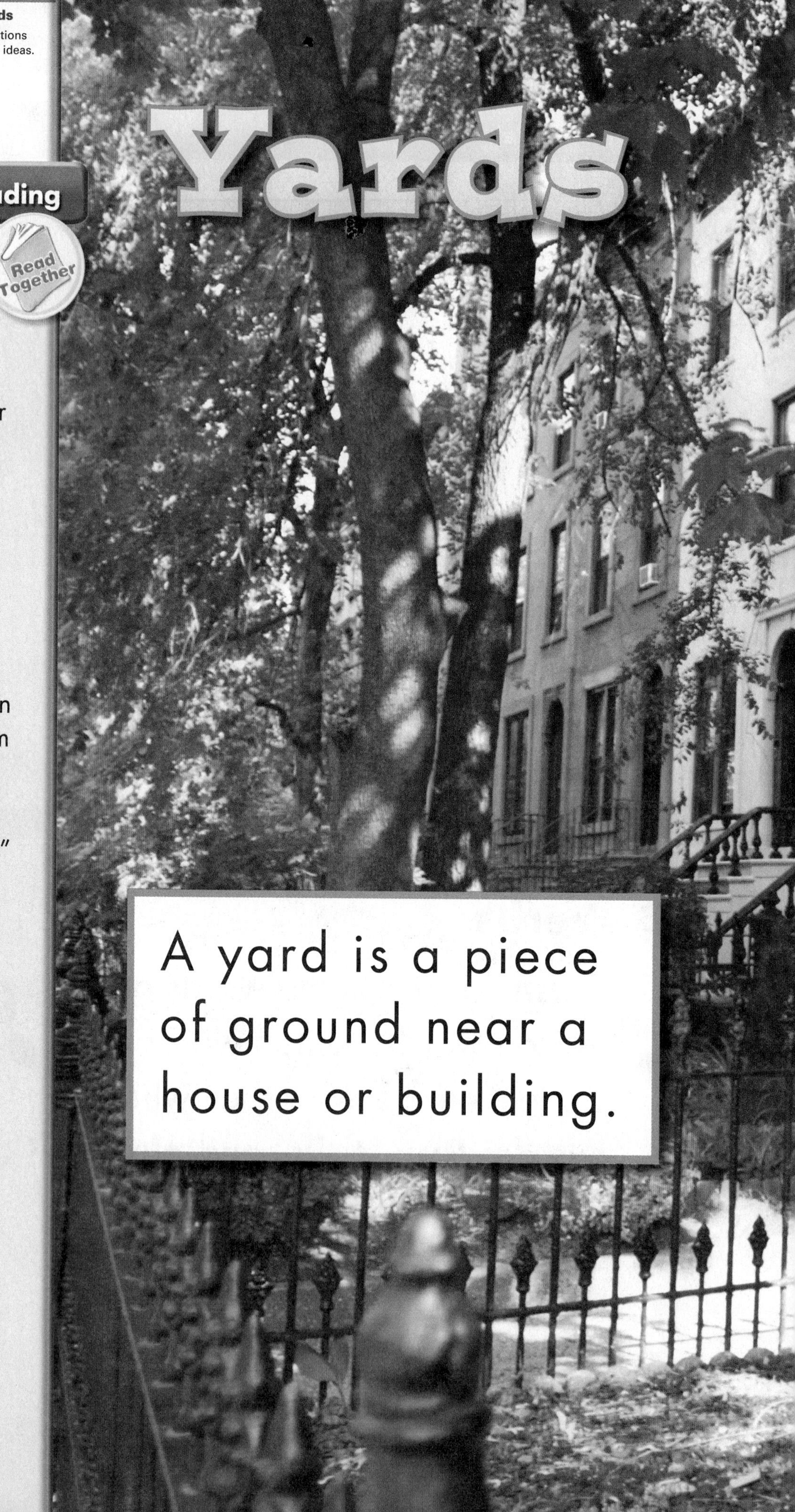

A yard is a piece of ground near a house or building.

Yards can be in the front or the back. A yard can be a nice place to play or relax.

Have you ever seen a yard like this?

Let's **Think** About...

How do these photos help readers understand what a yard is?
Photo Essay

Let's **Think** About...

Reading Across Texts Which yard shown in the photo essay "Yards" is most like the yard in the story *Tip and Tam?* How?

Writing Across Texts Draw pictures of things you might see in a yard. Use the selections to help you.

Common Core State Standards
Speaking/Listening 2. Ask and answer questions about key details in a text read aloud or information presented orally or through other media.
Also Language 1.a., 1.e.

READING STREET ONLINE
VOCABULARY ACTIVITIES
www.ReadingStreet.com

First I'll write my name on my paper. Then I'll write a sentence. I will circle the period at the end of my sentence.

Listening and Speaking

Restate instructions before you follow them.

Follow, Restate, Give Instructions We listen carefully to instructions we're given. Then we say them again, or restate them, to make sure we remember what we're supposed to do.

Practice It! Have a partner give you instructions. Restate the instructions, and then follow them. Say the verbs that tell what you do. Then you give instructions to your partner. Your partner should restate the directions and then follow them.

Vocabulary

A **noun** names a person, animal, place, or thing. A **verb** is a word that tells an action. We can sort nouns and verbs.

***Ball* is a noun.**

***Climb* is a verb.**

Practice It! Read the words. Identify and sort the nouns and verbs.

bed **hide** **man** **swim**

Handwriting

Proper Paper Position Be sure your paper is slanted correctly on your desk when you write. Write neatly, from left to right and from top to bottom. Look at the models on pages 174–175. Then write a row of these letters:

Ff **Bb** **Gg** **Ii**

Common Core State Standards

Language 5.c. Identify real-life connections between words and their use (e.g., note places at home that are *cozy*).

Oral Vocabulary

Let's Talk About

Read Together

Neighborhoods

- Share information about neighborhoods.
- Share ideas about what we can do with our neighborhood friends.

READING STREET ONLINE
CONCEPT TALK VIDEO
www.ReadingStreet.com

You've learned
0 2 2
Amazing Words
so far this year!

Common Core State Standards
Foundational Skills 2.c. Isolate and pronounce initial, medial vowel, and final sounds (phonemes) in spoken single-syllable words.

Let's Listen for

Read Together

Sounds

- Find five things that begin with the sound /d/. Say the sound.
- Find two things that end with the sound /l/. Say the sound.
- Find three things that begin with the sound /h/.
- Find three things that rhyme with *hop*. Say each sound in the word.

READING STREET ONLINE
SOUND-SPELLING CARDS
www.ReadingStreet.com

Play
Village

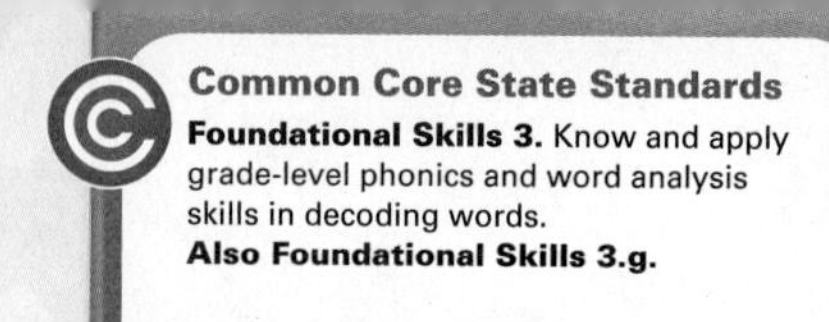

Phonics

Consonants *d, l*

Words I Can Blend

Words I Can Read

are

have

they

that

two

Sentences I Can Read

1. Are they in a can, Dad?
2. We have a sad cat.
3. Two did fill that big lid!

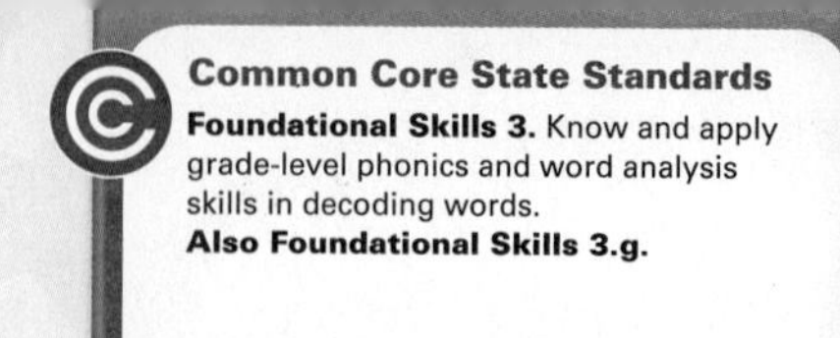
Common Core State Standards
Foundational Skills 3. Know and apply grade-level phonics and word analysis skills in decoding words.
Also Foundational Skills 3.g.

Phonics

Consonant *h*, Short *o*

Words I Can Blend

I Can Read!

I have a big doll. Doll can hop. Hop, Doll, hop! Doll can hop on a hill.

Two can look at Doll hop.

It got hot on that hill. The two got a hat. They are not hot.

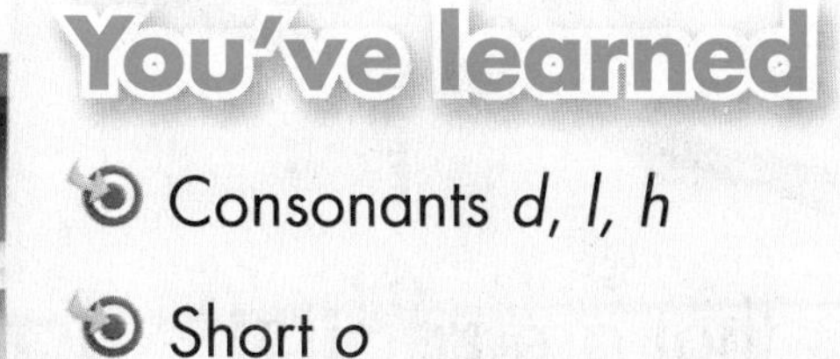

You've learned

- Consonants *d, l, h*
- Short *o*

High-Frequency Words

are have they that two

The Big Top

by Molly O'Keefe

illustrated by Hector Borlasca

Genre

Stories that are **realistic fiction** tell about events that could happen in the lives of real people and animals. This story is about two friends who play together.

Question of the Week

What can we do with our neighborhood friends?

Pam and Dot can hop and hop.

One, two. They can hop fast.

Dot and Pam sat.

Dot and Pam are on the mat.

A doll sat on the mat.

Tip hit the doll. Stop, Tip, stop!

A big top sat on the mat.

Tip can see it.

Dot got the big top.

Tip did not like that top!

Tip hid.

Dot and Pam sat.

Tip hit the big top.

Tip bit it. Stop, Tip, stop!

Pam and Dot stop Tip.

Pam and Dot have the big top.

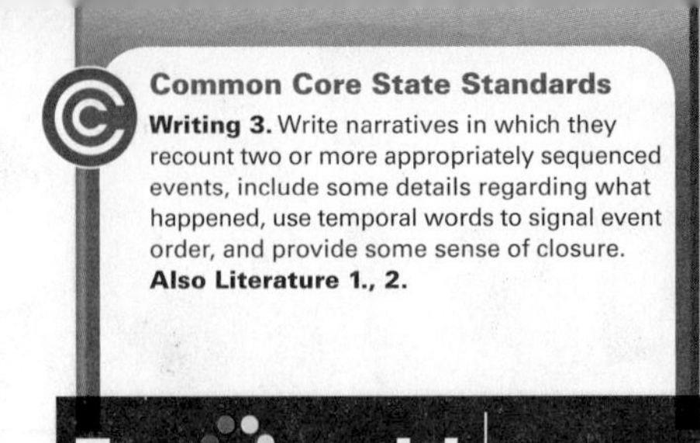
Common Core State Standards
Writing 3. Write narratives in which they recount two or more appropriately sequenced events, include some details regarding what happened, use temporal words to signal event order, and provide some sense of closure. **Also Literature 1., 2.**

Envision It! | Retell

READING STREET ONLINE
STORY SORT
www.ReadingStreet.com

Think Critically

1. Tip did not like the big top. Tell what you would do to help. **Text to Self**

2. Could this story really happen? Explain.

   Realism and Fantasy

3. **Look Back and Write** Look back at pages 98 and 99. What do Pam and Dot like to do? Write about it.

   Key Ideas and Details • Text Evidence

Meet the Illustrator

Hector Borlasca

Hector Borlasca loves to illustrate books because it brings a new surprise every day. He hopes that children see something new every time they look at his illustrations.

Here is another book illustrated by Hector Borlasca.

Use the Reading Log in the *Reader's and Writer's Notebook* to record your independent reading.

Common Core State Standards
Language 1.j. Produce and expand complete simple and compound declarative, interrogative, imperative, and exclamatory sentences in response to prompts.
Also Language 2.b.

Key Features of a Simple Sentence

- tells a complete idea
- begins with an uppercase letter
- can end with a period

READING STREET ONLINE
GRAMMAR JAMMER
www.ReadingStreet.com

Narrative

Simple Sentences

A **sentence** tells a complete idea. A sentence begins with an uppercase letter. Most sentences end with a period.

Writing Prompt Think about something a cat can do. Write a sentence about a cat. Tell what it does.

Writer's Checklist

Remember, you should . . .

- ✓ write about something a cat does.
- ✓ begin your sentence with an uppercase letter.
- ✓ end your sentence with a period. Say your sentence.

Student Model

The cat runs to the mat.

An uppercase, or capital, **T** begins the sentence.

This **sentence** tells what a cat does.

A **period** ends the sentence.

Conventions

Simple Sentences

Remember A sentence is a group of words that tells a complete idea. It begins with an uppercase letter. Many sentences end with a **period.**

Say this sentence.

Pam sat.

This is not a sentence.

Pam and Dot

Common Core State Standards
Informational Text 6. Distinguish between information provided by pictures or other illustrations and information provided by the words in a text.
Also Informational Text 7.

Social Studies in Reading

Read Together

Genre
Procedural Text

- Some selections use words along with signs and symbols.
- A sign tells you what to do.
- A symbol is a picture that stands for something else.
- Read "Around the Block." As you read, remember what you learned about signs and symbols.

Around the Block

There are many signs and symbols in our neighborhood.

Signs and symbols help us drive.

Signs and symbols help us ride.

Signs and symbols help keep us safe.

Let's Think About...

What signs and symbols do you see on these pages? **Procedural Text**

Let's Think About...

What do the signs and symbols tell you? **Procedural Text**

Let's Think About...

Reading Across Texts What kinds of street signs might Pam see in her neighborhood?

Writing Across Texts Draw a picture of some signs and symbols Pam might see in her neighborhood. Write a label for each.

Common Core State Standards

Speaking/Listening 1.a. Follow agreed-upon rules for discussions (e.g., listening to others with care, speaking one at a time about the topics and texts under discussion). **Also Speaking/Listening 1., 2., Language 1.a., 1.f.**

READING STREET ONLINE
VOCABULARY ACTIVITIES
www.ReadingStreet.com

Speak clearly when you give instructions.

Listening and Speaking

Give Instructions When we give instructions, we make sure to speak clearly. We make sure our instructions are easy to follow.

Practice It! Give a partner some simple instructions. Use sentences. Have your partner restate the instructions and follow them.

Vocabulary

Words that tell about or describe something are descriptive words, or **adjectives.** We can identify and sort adjectives that describe the way something looks, tastes, smells, feels, or sounds.

The word *sweet* describes how the grapes taste.

Practice It! Read these words. Write and say the words that tell how something feels.

rough **loud** **smooth** **spicy**

Handwriting

Proper Letter Size When you write, your letters should fit properly on the lines of your paper. Look at the models on pages 174–175. Then write a row of these letters:

Dd **Ll** **Hh** **Oo**

Use the models to write these words, being sure to leave space between the words:

doll **old** **hood**

Let's Talk About

Neighborhoods

- Share information about what is around us at school.
- Share ideas about what we do at school each day.

READING STREET ONLINE
CONCEPT TALK VIDEO
www.ReadingStreet.com

You've learned
0 3 0
Amazing Words
so far this year!

Common Core State Standards
Foundational Skills 2.c. Isolate and pronounce initial, medial vowel, and final sounds (phonemes) in spoken single-syllable words. **Also Foundational Skills 2., 2.b.**

Phonemic Awareness

Let's Listen for

Sounds

Read Together

- Find four things that begin with the sound /r/. Say the sound.
- Find three things that begin with the sound /w/. Say the sound.
- Find two things that begin with the sound /j/.
- Find two things that begin with the sound /k/.
- Find something that rhymes with *wet*. Say each sound in the word.

READING STREET ONLINE
SOUND-SPELLING CARDS
www.ReadingStreet.com

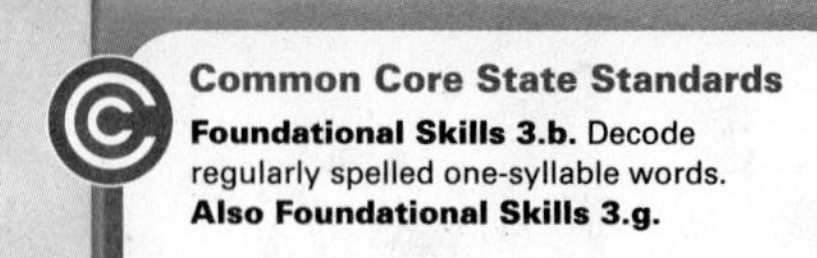

Phonics

Consonants *r, w, j*

Words I Can Blend

j a m

r a n

w i n

w i l l

r i m

Words I Can Read

he

is

to

with

three

Sentences I Can Read

1. He is in a jam.
2. Three ran to win.
3. Jim will sit on the rim with Jill.

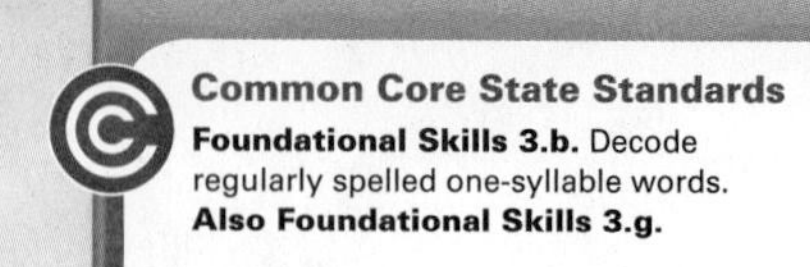
Common Core State Standards
Foundational Skills 3.b. Decode regularly spelled one-syllable words. **Also Foundational Skills 3.g.**

Phonics

Consonant *k*, Short *e*

Words I Can Blend

I Can Read!

Ken is three. He is a kid I met on a jet. Ken had a red bell with him.

Is a bell on a jet bad? Men on the jet tell Ken to sell that red bell. Will Ken get in a jam?

You've learned

- Consonants *r, w, j, k*
- Short *e*

High-Frequency Words

he is to with three

School Day

by Cass Stricker

illustrated by Hector Borlasca

Genre

In **realistic fiction,** the people and events are made up. Sam and his friends are made-up characters who do real things, like go to school.

Question of the Week

What is around us at school?

Sam is still in bed!

Mom will get him.

Grab the red bag, Sam!

Sam ran fast. He got on.

Sam sat with Fred.

Sam met Pat, Kim, and Jill.

The three tell the plan to Sam.

Pat did a jet kit. Jill will jig.

Kim will sit on a mat.

The red bag had a rip!

Fred will drop! Stop him!

Sam is sad. Kim will help him.

Jill and Pat will help him.

They will help Fred.

Sam is not sad.

Common Core State Standards

Literature 2. Retell stories, including key details, and demonstrate understanding of their central message or lesson.
Also Literature 1., Writing 3.

Envision It! | **Retell**

READING STREET ONLINE
STORY SORT
www.ReadingStreet.com

Think Critically

1. How is Sam's school like your school? **Text to Self**

2. What happens in the beginning of the story? What happens at the end?

Plot

3. Look Back and Write
Look back at page 128. What will Kim, Jill, and Pat do?

Key Ideas and Details • Text Evidence

School Bus

Friendly fellow
Dressed in yellow
Greets his kids
With a beep-beep hello!

by Dee Lillegard
illustrated by Dean MacAdam

Common Core State Standards
Language 1.f. Use frequently occurring adjectives.

Key Features of Sentences with Adjectives

- tell complete ideas
- describe people, places, animals, or things

READING STREET ONLINE
GRAMMAR JAMMER
www.ReadingStreet.com

Expressive

Sentences with Adjectives

A **sentence** tells a complete idea. Words that describe people, places, animals, or things are **adjectives.** A sentence may have an adjective or more than one adjective.

Writing Prompt Think about your favorite things. Write a sentence about one of them. Use an adjective to tell about the thing.

Writer's Checklist

Remember, you should ...

- ✓ write a sentence about a thing that you like.
- ✓ use an adjective to describe the thing.
- ✓ end the sentence with a period.

Student Model

I like my blue hat.

The sentence tells a complete idea.

The **adjective blue** tells about the hat.

A period ends the **sentence.**

Conventions

Adjectives

Some words tell more about people, places, animals, or things. Describing words are called **adjectives. Green, big, tall,** and **little** are adjectives. What other adjectives can you say?

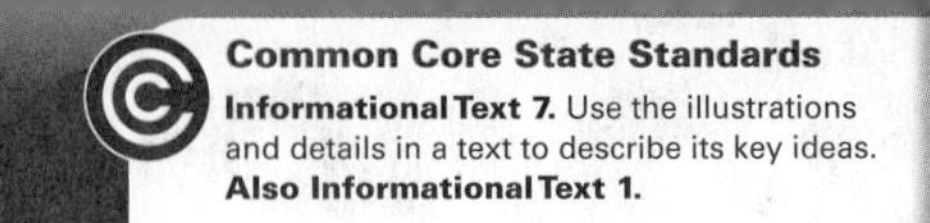
Common Core State Standards
Informational Text 7. Use the illustrations and details in a text to describe its key ideas. **Also Informational Text 1.**

Social Studies in Reading

Read Together

Genre
Photo Essay

- The words and photographs in a photo essay are about the same topic. The words tell and the photographs show.
- The photographs in a photo essay are usually memorable. The photographer wants you to feel as if you were there.
- Photographs help readers connect with real people, places, and events, even from different parts of the world.
- Read "How Do You Get to School?" Think about what you learned about photo essays.

How Do You Get to School?

Children go to school every day.
There are many ways to get to school.

Jelani walks to school.
Aisha rides a rickshaw.
How do you get to school?

Let's Think About...

How do you think the person who took these photographs wants you to feel?
Photo Essay

Let's Think About...

Reading Across Texts How does Sam in *School Day* get to school? How do the children shown in the photo essay get to school?

Writing Across Texts Draw pictures of the ways Sam and the children get to school. Label the pictures.

Common Core State Standards
Speaking/Listening 3. Ask and answer questions about what a speaker says in order to gather additional information or clarify something that is not understood. **Also Speaking/Listening 1.c., 2., Language 1.a., 1.f.**

READING STREET ONLINE
VOCABULARY ACTIVITIES
www.ReadingStreet.com

Get Ready For Grade 2

Ask questions if you don't understand a speaker.

Ask Questions If we're confused about something a speaker says, we ask him or her to explain.

Practice It! Have a partner tell you something. Listen carefully. Ask questions if you don't understand. Then tell something to your partner. When your partner asks you questions, listen carefully to each one so that you know exactly what your partner is asking. Then answer the questions.

Vocabulary

A descriptive word, or **adjective,** tells about people, animals, places, or things.

The word *little* describes the bird.

The little bird flies.

Practice It! Read these words. Write and say a descriptive word for each one.

bus **cat** **friend** **bike**

Handwriting

Proper Body Position Keep both feet flat on the floor when you write. Look at the models on pages 174–175. Then write a row of these letters:

Rr **Ww** **Jj** **Kk** **Ee**

Use the models to write these words, being sure to leave space between the words:

week **jar** **Kirk**

Common Core State Standards
Language 5.c. Identify real-life connections between words and their use (e.g., note places at home that are *cozy*).

Oral Vocabulary

Let's Talk About

Neighborhoods

- Share information about what we see around our neighborhood.
- Share ideas about places we can go and things we can do in our neighborhood.

READING STREET ONLINE
CONCEPT TALK VIDEO
www.ReadingStreet.com

You've learned
0 3 9
Amazing Words
so far this year!

Common Core State Standards
Foundational Skills 2.c. Isolate and pronounce initial, medial vowel, and final sounds (phonemes) in spoken single-syllable words. **Also Foundational Skills 2.b.**

Let's Listen for

Sounds

Read Together

- Find five things that begin with the sound /v/. Say the beginning sound.
- Find two things that begin with the sound /y/.
- Find three things that begin with the sound /z/.
- Find two things that rhyme with *hum*.
- Find two things that begin with the sound /kw/. Say each sound in one of those words.

READING STREET ONLINE
SOUND-SPELLING CARDS
www.ReadingStreet.com

Common Core State Standards
Foundational Skills 3. Know and apply grade-level phonics and word analysis skills in decoding words.
Also Foundational Skills 3.g.

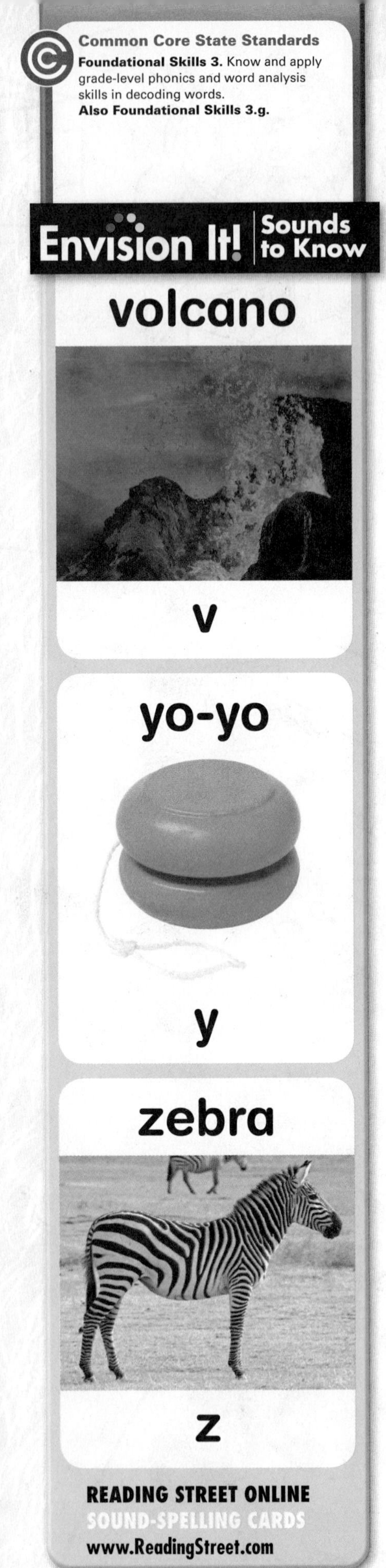

Phonics

Consonants v, y, z

Words I Can Blend

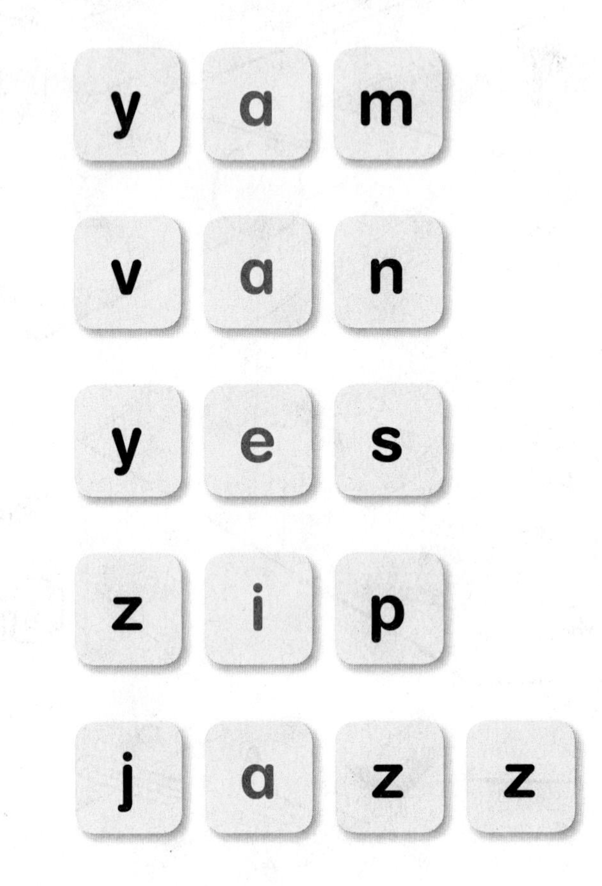

Words I Can Read

where

here

for

me

go

Sentences I Can Read

1. Yaz will get me the yam in the van.
2. Mom can zip it here.
3. Where can Val go for jazz?

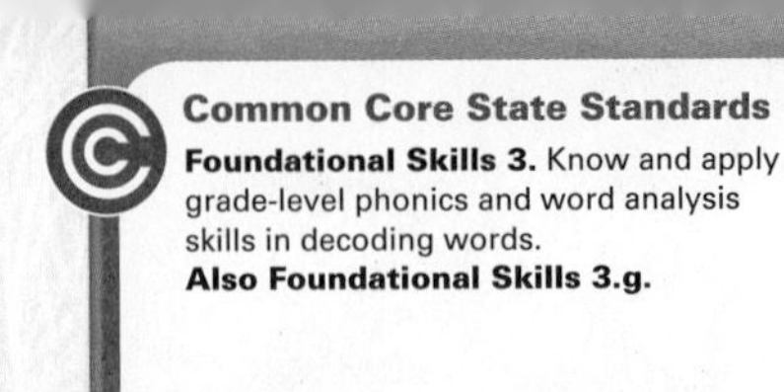

quilt

qu

umbrella

short u

READING STREET ONLINE
SOUND-SPELLING CARDS
www.ReadingStreet.com

Phonics

Consonant *qu*, Short *u*

Words I Can Blend

h u g

b u s

s u n

I Can Read!

Here is a quiz for us. Where can we go on a bus? A bus can get us to a vet. It can zip us to fun in the sun.

Yes, a bus will not quit. Get on a bus with me!

You've learned

- Consonants *v, y, z, qu*
- Short *u*

High-Frequency Words

where here for me go

Farmers Market

by Don Kent
illustrated by Hector Borlasca

Genre Events in **realistic fiction** could happen in real life. This story is about a farmers market that could be in a real neighborhood.

Read Together

Question of the Week

What can we see around our neighborhood?

Pam and Dad get on the bus.

Where will the bus go?

The bus will stop here.

Pam and Dad will have fun.

Look at Viv.

Viv will cut it. It is wet!

Look at Zak.

Zak will sell it.

Dad will get it.

Dad will set it in a bag and zip it.

Look at Bud.

Will you get a yam for me?

Dad and Pam get wet.

They will quit.

Dad and Pam got on the bus.

Dad and Pam had fun.

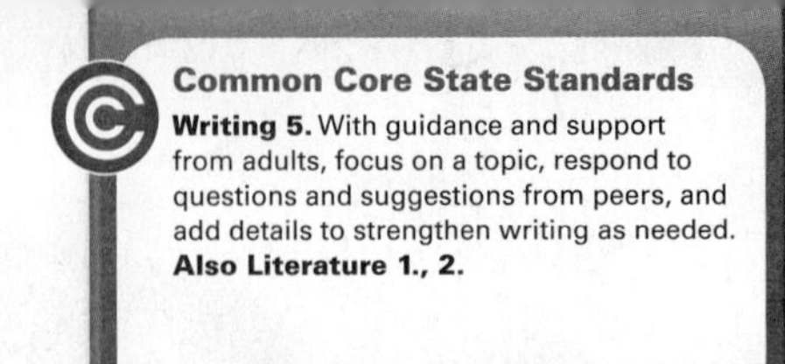
Common Core State Standards
Writing 5. With guidance and support from adults, focus on a topic, respond to questions and suggestions from peers, and add details to strengthen writing as needed. **Also Literature 1., 2.**

Envision It! | Retell

READING STREET ONLINE
STORY SORT
www.ReadingStreet.com

Think Critically

1. A farmers market is a place to buy fruits and vegetables. Name some other places where fruits and vegetables are sold. Text to World

2. Could this story really happen? Explain.

   Realism and Fantasy

3. **Look Back and Write** Look back at page 155. What can you buy at a farmers market? Write about it.

   Key Ideas and Details • Text Evidence

To Market, To Market

To market, to market,
To buy some sweet corn,
Home again, home again,
Blowing a horn!
To market, to market,
To buy tangerines,
Home again, home again,
Eating sardines!

illustrated by Debbie Palen

Common Core State Standards
Language 2. Demonstrate command of the conventions of standard English capitalization, punctuation, and spelling when writing. **Also Writing 2., Language 2.b.**

Key Features of Sentences with Nouns, Verbs, and Adjectives

- use nouns to tell about people, places, animals, or things
- use verbs to tell about actions
- use adjectives to describe people, places, animals, or things

READING STREET ONLINE
GRAMMAR JAMMER
www.ReadingStreet.com

Expository

Sentences with Nouns, Verbs, and Adjectives

A **sentence** tells a complete idea. A sentence has a verb. Most sentences have a noun. A sentence may have an adjective.

Writing Prompt Think about where you and your family buy food. Write about the place. Use a noun, a verb, and an adjective in your sentence.

Writer's Checklist

Remember, you should . . .

- ✓ use a noun in your sentence to name a place.
- ✓ use a verb to tell about an action.
- ✓ use an adjective to describe something.

Student Model

The market sells big apples.

The **noun market** names the place.

The **verb sells** tells about an action.

The **adjective big** describes the apples.

Conventions

Sentences

A **sentence** tells a complete idea. It begins with an uppercase letter. Many sentences end with a period. A sentence has a noun and a verb. It can have adjectives to describe. What sentence can you say?

A man likes green beans.

Common Core State Standards
Literature 2. Retell stories, including key details, and demonstrate understanding of their central message or lesson.
Also Literature 1., 5., 7.

Social Studies in Reading

Read Together

Genre
Fable

- A fable is a short story that teaches a lesson.
- Characters in fables usually learn a lesson from the mistakes they make.
- The author wants readers to connect a fable's lesson to their personal experiences.
- Read "The Maid and the Milk Pail." Think about what you've learned about fables as you read.

The Maid and the Milk Pail

A girl took milk to a market. She thought, "I will sell this milk. I will buy a lovely new dress."

The girl let go of the pail. It fell. Now the girl could not buy a dress.

Lesson: Don't count on getting something until you actually have it.

Let's Think About...

What mistake does the girl make? **Fable**

Let's Think About...

What lesson does the girl learn? How can you connect this lesson to something that happened to you? **Fable**

Let's Think About...

Reading Across Texts When do *Farmers Market* and "The Maid and the Milk Pail" take place? Where do they take place? How do you know?

Writing Across Texts Why are Pam and Dad in *Farmers Market* going to a market? Why is the girl in "The Maid and the Milk Pail" going to a market? Write about their reasons.

Common Core State Standards
Speaking/Listening 4. Describe people, places, things, and events with relevant details, expressing ideas and feelings clearly. **Also Speaking/Listening 6., Language 1.a., 5.a.**

Read Together

Let's Learn It!

READING STREET ONLINE
VOCABULARY ACTIVITIES
www.ReadingStreet.com

First, my dad and I went to a farmers market. Then we bought some oranges. Last, we went home and ate them.

Listening and Speaking

Get Ready For Grade 2

Use words such as *first, next,* and *last* when you tell a story.

Relate an Experience in Sequence

When we tell about something that happened to us, we use words such as *first, then, next,* and *last* so that listeners will understand.

Practice It! Think of something that happened to you. Tell others about it. Speak in complete sentences.

Vocabulary

A **noun** is a word that names people, animals, places, or things. We can sort nouns into categories of people, animals, things, and places.

Practice It! Read these words. Identify and sort them into categories of people, animals, things, and places.

dog **box** **boy** **home**

Handwriting

Self-Evaluation During and after writing, make sure your letters are neatly written and formed correctly. Look at the models on pages 174–175. Then write a row of these letters: **Vv** **Yy** **Zz** **Uu** **Qq**

Use the models to write these sentences. Leave enough space between the words and sentences.

Val has a quiz. Val and Quin study.

My Family

mom
mama
mother
mommy
sister
daughter
dad
papa
father
daddy
This is me!
These are my relatives.
brother
son

cousin
uncle
aunt

baby
grandpa
grandfather
grandma
grandmother

My Home

bookshelf

books

toys

bed

microwave
stove
sink
refrigerator
counter
desk 
chair
couch
carpet

The Market

Canne
Sou
shelves
aisle

milk
cheese

banana
grapes
apple

lettuce
tomatoes
carrots

Sam

a
green
I
see

Tip and Tam

do
look
was
yellow
you

Snap!

like
one
the
we

The Big Top

are
have
that
they
two

Farmers Market

for
go
here
me
where

School Day

he
is
three
to
with

Aa Bb Cc

Dd Ee Ff

Gg Hh Ii

Jj Kk Ll

Mm Nn Oo

Pp Qq Rr

Ss Tt Uu

Vv Ww Xx

Yy Zz

Acknowledgments

Text

Grateful acknowledgment is made to the following for copyrighted material:

Alfred A. Knopf, Inc., A Division of Random House, Inc. & BookStop Literary Agency, LLC

"School Bus" from *Go! Poetry in Motion* by Dee Lillegard. Copyright © 2006 by Dee Lillegard. Used by permission.

BookStop Literary Agency, LLC

"Bedroom Window" from *Wake Up House! Rooms Full of Poems* by Dee Lillegard. Copyright © 2000 by Dee Lillegard. Used by permission of BookStop Literary Agency, LLC.

Elizabeth M. Hauser

"My Family" from *Rhymes About Us* by Marchette Chute. Copyright © 1974 by E.P. Dutton & Co., Inc.

Note: Every effort has been made to locate the copyright owner of material reproduced on this component. Omissions brought to our attention will be corrected in subsequent editions.

Cover: (B) ©Theo Allots/Getty Images, (T) Getty Images

Illustrations

EI2–EI5 Mary Anne Lloyd

EI8–EI17 Chris Lensch

14 Suwin Chan

18 - 27, 45 - 53, 70 - 83, 96 - 122, 125 - 150, 152 - 157 Hector Borlasca

29 Amy Cartwright

32, 33 Nan Brooks

40 Aaron Zenz

55 Wednesday Kirwan

66 Mary Sullivan

94 Miki Sakamoto

95 Lane Gregory

122 Karol Kaminski

150 Stacy Curtis

159 Debbie Palen

162, 163 Luciana Navarro Powell

Photographs

Every effort has been made to secure permission and provide appropriate credit for photographic material. The publisher deeply regrets any omission and pledges to correct errors called to its attention in subsequent editions.

Unless otherwise acknowledged, all photographs are the property of Pearson Education, Inc.

Photo locators denoted as follows: Top (T), Center (C), Bottom (B), Left (L), Right (R), Background (Bkgd)

CVR Theo Allots/Getty Images; **4** Fuse/Thinkstock; **10** Fuse/Thinkstock; **13** (BR) Monkey Business/Fotolia; **16** (BL) GRIN/NASA; **16** (TCR) Jack Fields/Photo Researchers; **16** (TL) Robert Huberman/Superstock; **16** (BCL) Jupiter Images; **35** (TR) Frank Lukasseck/Getty Images; **35** (TL) Jeremy Woodhouse/Getty Images; **35** (TC) Vrabelpeter1/Fotolia; **36** (Bkgrd) Masterfile Corporation; **40** (BL) Erik Dreyer/Getty Images; **42** Kurhan/Fotolia; **58** Mark Leibowitz/Corbis; **59** (B) JGI/Jamie Grill/Blend Images/Getty Images ; **59** (T) Paul Barton/Corbis; **61** Ellen McKnight/Alamy; **62** (BL) Thinkstock; **62** (Bkgrd) Ariel Skelley/Corbis; **63** Masterfile Corporation; **66** (CL) Rudi Von Briel/PhotoEdit; **66** (TL) Andersen Ross/Photodisc/Getty Images; **68** ©Premaphotos/Nature Picture Library; **84** Stockbyte/Jupiter Images; **85** (T) Bambu Productions/Getty Images; **85** (B) Peter Ravallo/Alamy; **86** John Giustina/Photodisc/Getty Images; **87** (TR) Steffan Hill/Alamy; **88** Jupiter Images; **89** (CR) Blend Images/Getty Images; **89** (BR) Jupiter Images; **94** (TL) Terie Rakke/Getty Images; **94** (CL) Vittorio Bruno/Shutterstock; **111** (T) Mike Clarke/Getty Images; **111** (B) Kim Karpeles/Alamy; **113** Getty Images; **114** Masterfile Corporation; **115** (CR) Masterfile Corporation; **115** (BR) Blend Images/Jupiter Images; **118** (TL) NASA; **118** (CL) AbleStock/Photolibrary/Getty Images; **120** (B) Carleton Chinner/Shutterstock; **136** Anders Ryman/Corbis; **137** (CL) Rafiqur Rahman/Reuters/Corbis; **137** (TC) ©Frans Lemmens/Getty Images; **138** SW Productions/Getty Images; **139** Juniors Bildarchiv/Alamy; **140** (BC) David Grossman/Alamy; **140** (Bkgrd) Heide Benser/zefa/Corbis; **140** (TC) BlueOrange Studio/Fotolia; **144** (BL) Tr3gi/Fotolia; **144** (TL) G. Brad Lewis/Getty Images; **168** (BL) Abode/Beateworks/Corbis; **168** (BR) Arcaid/Alamy; **168** (Bkgrnd) Alamy; **169** (B) Elliott Kaufman/Beateworks/Corbis; **169** (T) Getty Images; **170** (TR) Naka/Fotolia; **170** (Bkgrd) Blue Jean Images/Alamy; **171** (Bkgrd) Getty Images; **171** (BR) D. Hurst/Alamy.

High-Frequency Words

Identify and read the high-frequency words that you have learned. How many words can you read?

Unit R.1
a
green
I
see

Unit R.2
like
one
the
we

Unit R.3
do
look
was
yellow
you

Unit R.4
are
have
that
they
two

Unit R.5
he
is
three
to
with

Unit R.6
for
go
here
me
where

Unit 1.1
come
in
my
on
way

Unit 1.2
she
take
up
what

Unit 1.3
blue
from
get
help
little
use

Unit 1.4
eat
five
four
her
this
too

Unit 1.5
saw
small
tree
your

Unit 1.6
home
into
many
them

Unit 2.1
catch
good
no
put
said
want

Unit 2.2
be
could
horse
of
old
paper

Unit 2.3
live
out
people
who
work

Unit 2.4
down
inside
now
there
together

Unit 2.5
around
find
food
grow
under
water

Unit 2.6
also
family
new
other
some
their

Unit 3.1
always
become
day
everything
nothing
stays
things

Unit 3.2
any
enough
ever
every
own
sure
were

Unit 3.3
away
car
friends
house
our
school
very

Unit 3.4
afraid
again
few
how
read
soon

Unit 3.5
done
know
push
visit
wait

Unit 3.6
before
does
good-bye
oh
right
won't

Unit 4.1
about
enjoy
give
surprise
worry
would

Unit 4.2
colors
draw
drew
great
over
show
sign

Unit 4.3
found
mouth
once
took
wild

Unit 4.4
above
eight
laugh
moon
touch

Unit 4.5
picture
remember
room
stood
thought

Unit 4.6
across
because
dance
only
opened
shoes
told

Unit 5.1
along
behind
eyes
never
pulling
toward

Unit 5.2
door
loved
should
wood

Unit 5.3
among
another
instead
none

Unit 5.4
against
goes
heavy
kinds
today

Unit 5.5
built
early
learn
science
through

Unit 5.6
answered
carry
different
poor